Before I Arrive

This handbook is written based on personal experience; the information should be used as you see fit, as your circumstances may not be the same and you should adjust your use of the information accordingly.

First published in 2013 by Adoption UK Linden House, 55 The Green, South Bar Street, Banbury, OX16 9AB
http://www.adoptionuk.org/

The right of H Townsend to be illustrated as author and illustrator of this work has been asserted by her in accordance with the Copyright, Designs and Patents Act, 1988

'Bigger, stronger, wiser, kind' reproduced with the kind permission of Circle of Security www.circleofsecurity.net

Printed and bound in Great Britain by Hobbs the Printers Ltd, Totton, Hampshire
ISBN: 978-0-95159506-0

For Mum, Dad, Lorraine & Keith. Thank you for your love, support and bravery in helping us on our journey to becoming a forever family.

About Me

It might take a little time before I can trust you enough to accept that you love me and to show you that I care about what you think of me.

It also might take me some time before I am ready to visit your house; so while you are waiting for me to be ready, it will help my parent/s and me if you understand how your behaviour and feelings will influence my behaviour and feelings.

My Journey So Far

Please don't tell people that I am adopted, this is my journey to understand and share so my parent/s and me need to choose if and when we are comfortable to tell people.

I will tell you what I want people to know about my journey in my own time. If someone does know and asks you why I was adopted, then please tell them that my mummy or daddy will have to answer any questions; it is important my trust is not broken.

My Birth Family

Please don't be negative about my birth family; I still love them even though I can't live with them anymore and I have a big enough heart that I can love you all. Please don't tell me how lucky I am to have a new family as I might still want to be with my old family and being adopted isn't lucky – it's necessary so I can be safe and loved.

If I ask a question about my birth family and you don't know the answer, please tell me that you don't know but you will write down the question and give it to mummy or daddy so they can try to find out the answer for me.

My Feelings

Sometimes the more horrible I am being, the more I am feeling very messy inside and I need you even more than when I am behaving well. When my behaviour seems bad, it actually means that I need you to stay calm, take charge and be firm but kind to me.

I sometimes don't know what to do with a big feeling and I need your help to manage it. I might not have learnt how to feel angry or frustrated or even happy so you will have to help me understand what I am feeling by verbalising my behaviour.

You might say 'I can see you are feeling very angry, what are you feeling angry about?' You could show me how to do big roaring fiery lion noises when I'm cross, as a way of expressing my anger or frustration.

My Feelings

Sometimes I might push you to act like my birth family as this is all I know; please remain calm with me and I will learn that family life is meant to be a warm, safe and loving place.

Sometimes my feelings might get too big and I might shout at you and tell you that you are not my 'real' grandparent/aunt/uncle'. I need you to stay calm and tell me that you are my 'real' grandparent/aunt/uncle and that you love me very much.

If anything worries you about my behaviour, please remember to tell my mummy or daddy so they can help me with it.

My Feelings

Shouting 'No' or 'Don't' might remind me of scary times. If you can remember it would be more helpful to ask me to do something correctly like 'Please Walk' instead of 'No Running'. If you do say 'No' please say it in a calm, firm tone. It's OK if you forget this sometimes; I just need you to try so I can learn I am in a safe environment.

When you are teaching me what is right, make me feel like I belong by saying 'in our family we ....'

Straight after a tantrum is when I will be most open to let you hug me and talk to me about how I am feeling.

A Big Feeling

When I feel I can trust you, I might share something that seems alarming or scary. Please don't tell me that what I am feeling is wrong or not important. 'Acknowledge' that you have understood what I have told you and ask me 'what' made me feel like that? I may then be ready for you to try and help me work out this big feeling.

When the big feeling that I have shared with you has resulted in unsafe or unacceptable behaviour, I need a consequence that I can learn from - not a punishment. For instance if I have drawn on the wall the consequence will be that I need to clean the wall, even if it is with your help. A punishment will not work with me as I may not have been taught what happens when I do something wrong; instead I need to have a logical consequence to my behaviour. If you have 'acknowledged' and 'asked' me about my big feeling, I may be more accepting of my consequence as I will feel that you have listened to me.

Getting Close To You

My parent/s may ask you not to pick me up, hug or comfort me when I first arrive as I am learning that I belong to them and that I can trust in them for everything; it is very important I attach to them first.

When I am ready I would like lots of hugs and to hear how proud you are that I am a part of your family. It's OK if it takes you some time to love me, it will take me time too. In the meantime practice saying 'I love you' to me and one day I might be able to say it back.

It will help me to feel part of the family if you tell me funny stories and show me pictures of when my mummy or daddy were little! Hang pictures of me on your wall before I come to your house for the first time, as this will really make me feel I belong.

Doing Things Together

Exercise will produce positive chemicals that will help me to be happy. A group activity will also help me feel part of the family:

- Swimming
- Walking and picnics in the woods
- Going to the zoo
- Paddling at the beach

I may not have been to these places before though so I might get a little overwhelmed and want or need to go home sooner than you think.

Doing Things Together - One on One

Regular planned special time with you by myself will help us learn to trust each other and can get me used to your company:

- Dancing round the kitchen
- Blowing bubbles
- Mutual face painting
- Going to the park or beach
- Reading a story
- Cooking
- Painting using our hands
- Play dough
- Jigsaws

I need a verbal countdown 5 minutes before the activity we are doing is about to come to an end as this may cut down on a potential tantrum. Maybe we could count down to the end of the activity together?

Praise

Praising me will develop my self-esteem and behaviour; I might not feel like I am important so praising me is a good way of changing this. I might not believe it the first few times you say it - let me overhear you say something nice about me; I might believe you more if I think you don't know I am there.

Please be specific when you praise me so I can believe you are being sincere. If I have done something I am proud of please share in my excitement as I am learning how to feel a sense of accomplishment. Please praise me for commonplace behaviour; I might be really good at washing my hands when I go to the toilet so please don't forget to praise me when I do this. Please praise me for my behaviour or my handling of a big emotion when I leave your house. If you can tell my parent/s in front of me this will help me believe what you are saying is true.

Being Different To My Cousins

You might think that it doesn't matter that I am different but I might get worried that I don't look the same as the other children in the family; this might make me feel like I don't belong. I might need to talk about the differences and learn to be ok with them.

Telling me it doesn't matter will make me feel worse; instead find a way to celebrate my differences.

My Routine

Although it will be a while before I am ready for you to baby-sit me, it is important that you know that my routine is very important to me as I need structure to help my brain grow.

Please make sure I have my lunch and snacks at the time my mummy or daddy have asked. My brain is too fragile for stimulants so please do not give me coke or sweets two hours before bedtime or before my meals. If I don't eat very much it's OK, just tell my mummy or daddy later on so they know.

It will make me really happy and learn to believe what you say is true, when you remember simple things such as buying my favourite sandwich filling or my favourite cereal for when I visit.

Special Nurture Times

My bedtime will be my special time and it is very important to me. I need a story, lots of cuddles (if I am ready for this) and gazing into and touching each other's faces.

It helps if you talk to me about my day in soft, constant tones. If it has been a tricky day for me then please talk to me openly about this and praise me for working out how I was feeling.

Most of all I need you to be

Bigger, Stronger, Wiser & Kind